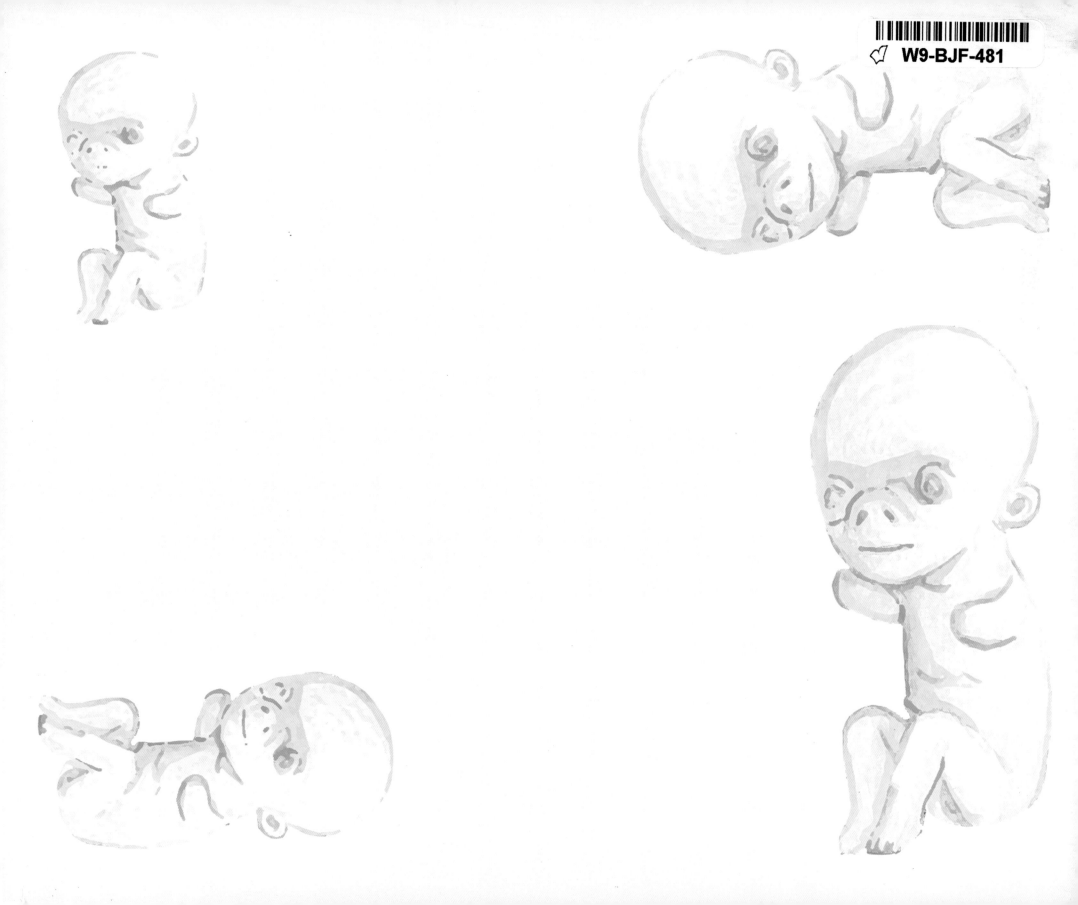

Disabilities?!

Soul Vision Works Publishing
P.O.Box 360063
Brooklyn, New York 11236
www.soulvisionworks.com

*This book is dedicated to my Mother, Rahil Taalibat,
whose love and encouragement inspires me to face adversity
with wisdom, courage, strength, and perseverance.*

Library of Congress Cataloging-in Publication Data

Vision, Mutiya Sahara, 1969-
    Disabilities?1 / written by Mutiya Vision ; pictures by Ignacio Alcantara.
      p. cm.
    Summary: A boy with no arms but a positive outlook focuses on developing his
mind, meeting new challenges, and loving himself.
    ISDN 0-9659538-9-0 (all. paper)
    [1. People with disabilities--Fiction. 2. Self-perception--Fiction. 3. Stories in rhyme.] I.
Alcantara, Ignacio, ill. Ip. Title.

PS8.3.V763Did 2004
[E]--dc22

Manufactured in China

Disabilities?!

Written By Mutiya Vision
Pictures By Ignacio Alcantara

Soul Vision Works Publishing  New York

*It
gave God great
pleasure to create me!*

*In God's eye, I am a
trophy of great
beauty.*

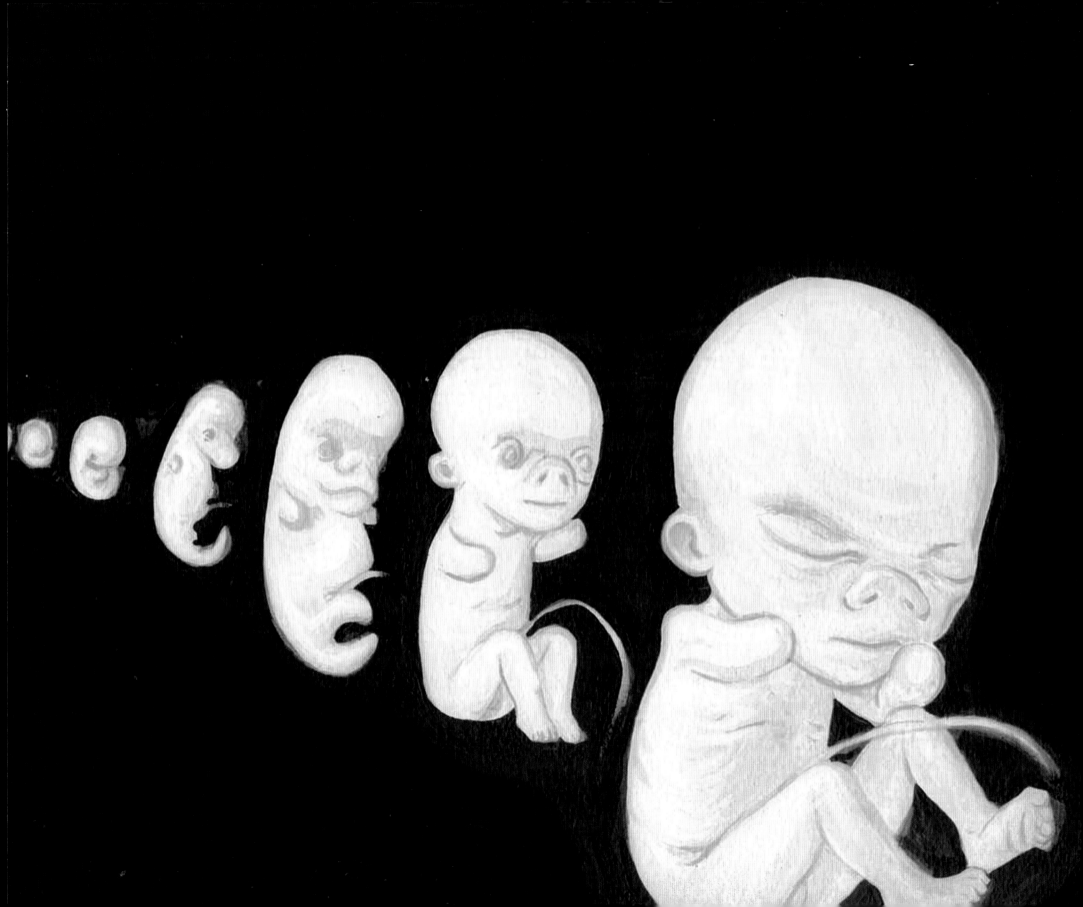

*I was
crafted to
perfection,
sculptured by
God's own hand.*

*Every curve was fine
tuned to a divine
master
plan.*

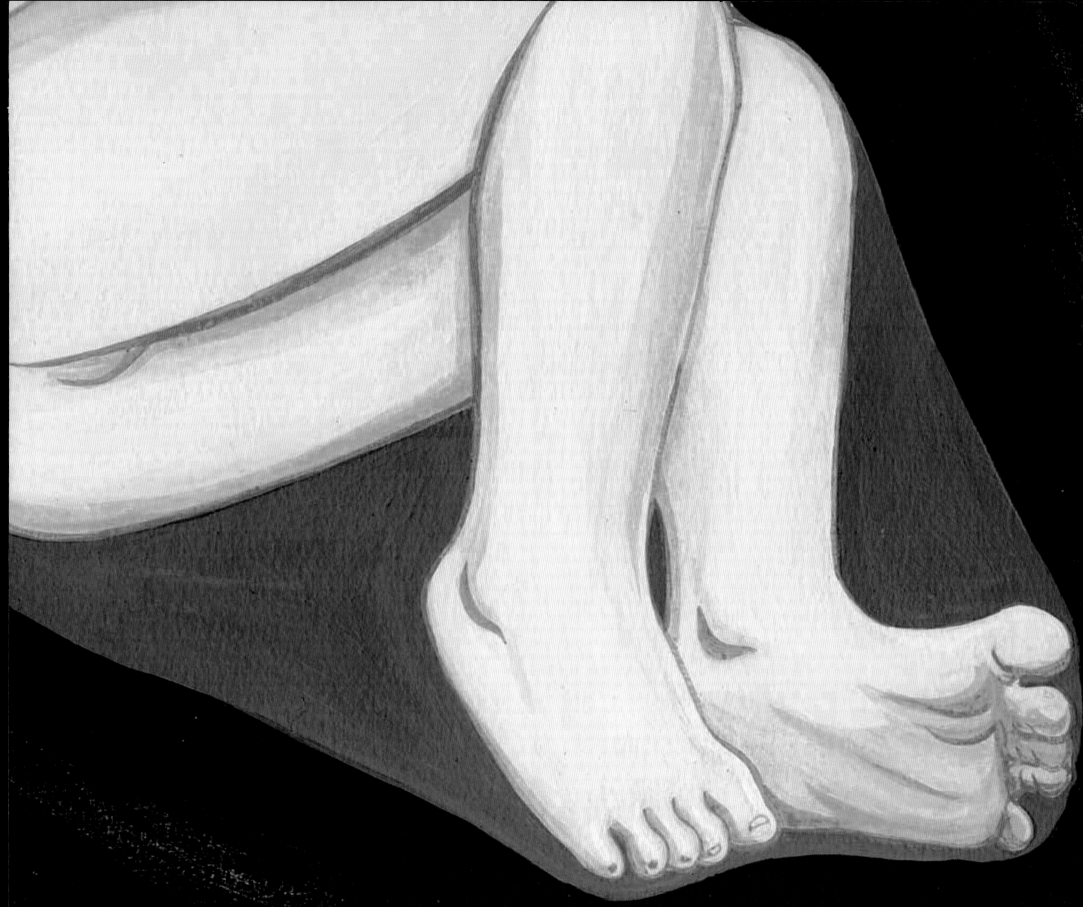

*From
thought to creation
I am now official,
a creature born
to be very
special.*

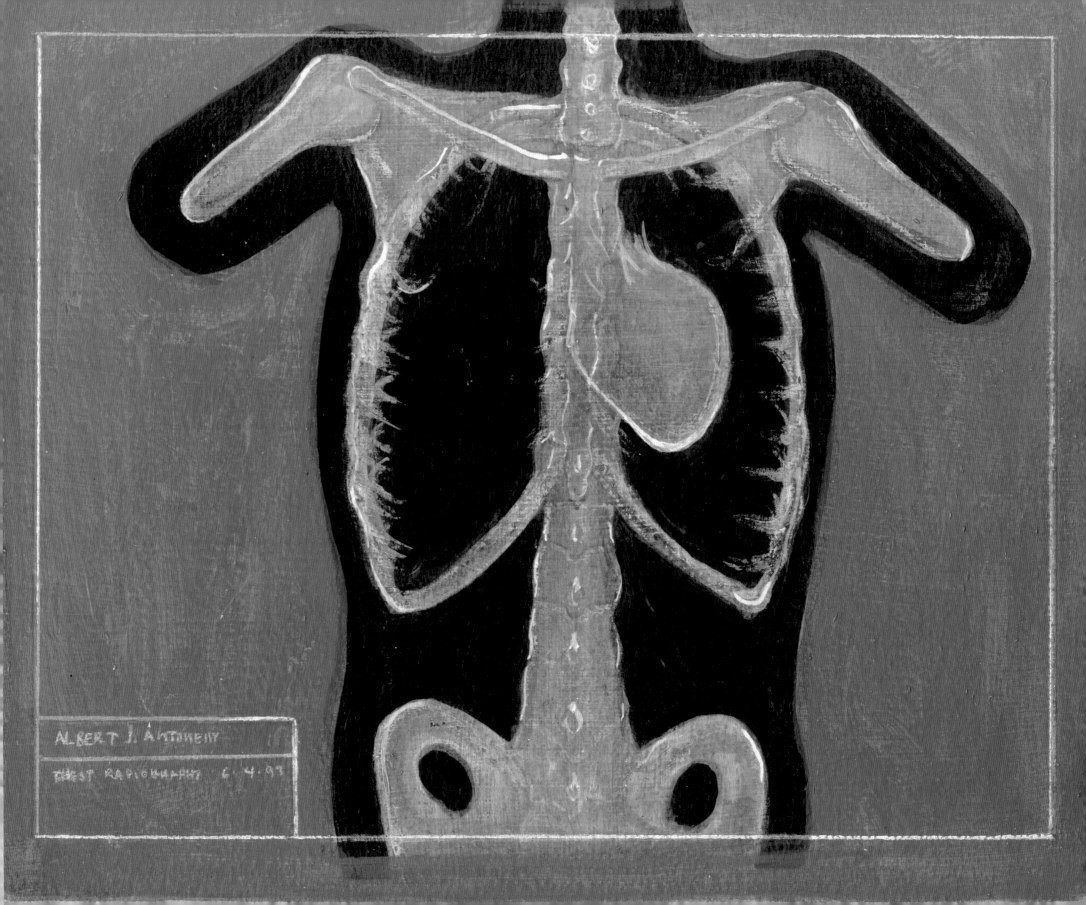

ALBERT J. ANTHONY

CHEST RADIOGRAPHY   6·4·07

*I felt ashamed
and did not want
to be me.*

*I now know
I'm a miracle,
not some
tragedy!*

*But
average humans
don't understand!*

*So they let their
ignorance have
the upper
hand.*

*Beauty
is in the eye of
the beholder, that's true.*

*The only sight that really
matters is that
beauty within
you!*

If you enjoyed reading this book, you'll want to add other
Soul Vision Works books to your special collection.
Look out for these titles:

Daddy Loves His Baby Girl
The Sister Who Copied Me
Adapt
Only You Can Make You Happy
My Very Breast Friend
Missing You
If Only I Could
What Makes Me Beautiful?
Who's That Crying?
Practice Makes Perfect
Isn't There anything Here With A Yes On It?

Get all these and much, much more on the web at:
www.soulvisionworks.com